ACKNOWLEDGEMENTS

Many thanks to Julie and Blake Carpenter and George Weinstein for
their help, support and encouragement in producing this document.

Cover by: Budget Book Design

whitehall printing company

GRAYWATER RESOURCE INC.
POB 2588
Suwanee, GA 30024-0982

www.graywaterresource.com

Contents

Section 1

Section 2

Section 3

SECTION 1

Graywater

Water shortages, droughts, increased populations and...beautiful landscapes? Can these things really go together? This publication will explain what graywater is, how it can be used and why we should be tapping into this neglected resource. Graywater can help maintain the beauty of residential and commercial landscapes as the pressure increases to move other water resources away from all but the most necessary functions. Even more importantly, graywater can save homeowners with a septic system from the expense and trauma that accompanies drainfield failure.

By definition, graywater is any wastewater that has not been contaminated by sewage or food preparation. Graywater usually comes from clothes laundry, showers, bathtubs, and bathroom and laundry sinks. (Laundry water from soiled diapers should never go into a graywater system.)

The term graywater is often mistakenly used for the tertiary treated liquid which is pumped from waste treatment facilities. Tertiary treated effluent is often used for landscape irrigation such as golf courses.

Black water is the term used to describe sewage from toilets, urinals, bidets, and areas where food is prepared or disposed. The main differences between graywater and black water is that black water has far more nitrogen in the form of nitrates or nitrides. Much of the bacteria contained in black water is a significant source of human pathogens or disease-carrying bacteria.

The use of graywater in the U.S. became popular about 30 years ago in California, because of extreme drought conditions and the great population increase in the western coastal region. Today, the problems of water shortages due to drought conditions and increased population are popping up all over the country.

The Advantages of Using Graywater

America began the 20th century with an average person consuming about 5 gallons of water per day. This included laundry, cooking, drinking and occasionally bathing. Water usually had to be drawn up from a well, then taken into the house in buckets. The same water often served the entire family for baths. Since there were no drains in most homes, any water carried into the house had to be taken back outside, where it would be used to water gardens. In today's society, with easy access to clean water, each of us consumes between 50 and 100 gallons of water per day, while reclaiming less than 1% of graywater.

The water shortages and watering restrictions we have today can only become worse. During the past 30 years, the U.S. population has increased by 52%, while the demand for fresh water has increased 300%. **The future need for fresh water is expected to double every 20 years.** With water supplies barely meeting the needs of many communities today, our ways of using water will change dramatically over the next 20 years. In some parts of the country, as much as half of the water used today is for outdoor watering. Much of the water used for outdoor watering can be replaced with graywater. Graywater is virtually an untapped source of landscape water for the private homeowner.

A graywater recovery system can be a great insurance policy against drought and watering restrictions for the homeowner. The value of plants and trees at many private residences today can exceed 20% of the total property value. The average home generates enough graywater to sustain most private landscapes. Each week a family of four will generate approximately 1000 gallons of graywater from showers, baths, and laundry. The laundry alone will generate nearly 50 gallons of graywater per washer load.

A graywater system can extend the life of a septic system or may allow a failing drainfield to recover by reducing the amount of sewage flowing into it.

Graywater systems can greatly reduce the amount of sewage going into waste treatment plants while reducing the amount of nitrogen and phosphorus being pumped into our fresh water reservoirs.

Anatomy of Graywater

Graywater is more than 99% water and less than 1% organic material and soil. The organic material typically consists of detergent and fillers, micro-fibers, salt, body oils, hair and skin follicles and dirt from laundry and bathing. Most of these organic particles are microscopic in size, which allows them to be broken down very quickly by bacteria. Much of the liquid entering a graywater system is warm, which helps to accelerate the rate of bacteria growth and the rate at which the organic particles are being broken down. Because of the rapid increase of bacteria in graywater, most states do not allow it to be stored for more than a few hours, or dispersed on the soil surface without being filtered and treated with chemicals for sanitizing. Filtering and sanitizing graywater is not overly complex since graywater has many of the same properties as the water in swimming pools.

Filtering graywater is much the same as filtering pool water. A sand filter is ideal for removing most of the organic particles, hair, and micro-fibers. Graywater should always be filtered before it goes into a storage tank or is pumped by an irrigation pump or through a sprinkler system, to prevent them from failing due to buildup of hair and micro-fibers.

Note: More details on filters are given in Section 2 on Graywater Components.

When sanitizing graywater, it is best to break away from the traditional home swimming pool method of sanitizing. Chlorine is the chemical of choice for pool sanitation by the average homeowner, because you can buy it almost anywhere, it's cheap and everybody knows a little about it. Chlorine is an effective sanitizer, but over a very narrow pH range (between 7.2 and 7.6). In a swimming pool, it is easy to maintain the proper pH range with chemicals because the water is not continually replaced. In a graywater system the liquid is continually being replaced and the pH range is altered by soaps and detergents, to the point that chlorine is often ineffective. Chlorine can also be somewhat damaging to vegetation. Bromine or ozone generators are better choices for graywater sanitation.

Bromine can be found in stabilized tablet form through most swimming pool supply stores. Although the initial cost per pound is more for bromine than chlorine, bromine lasts longer so the end cost is about the same. Bromine is less stressful to plants than chlorine. In fact some horticulturalist suggest using bromine with irrigation systems in plant nurseries to prevent things like root rot. When bromine is applied to the soil surface through irrigation, it is broken down by sunlight at the rate of about 60% during the first 24 hours, so there is very little residual effect.

Note: More information about bromine and ozone generators can be found in Section 2 on Graywater Components.

Not all graywater systems need filters or chemicals for sanitation. The ideal graywater system is completely sub-terrain, using a minimum of components and gravity to distribute graywater near the soil surface where it can be effectively treated by beneficial bacteria. About 90% of soil bacteria live within the top 18 inches of the surface or topsoil. The topsoil environment is rich in oxygen, bacteria, nematodes and earthworms which work in harmony to breakdown the organic particles in graywater into microscopic elements which can be absorbed by plant roots as fertilizer. Also when graywater is distributed sub-terrain, there is less evaporation, so plants can make better use of it.

Note: See Sections 2 and 3 for complete details on graywater components and systems.

Graywater is loaded with nutrients, which plants love. Most laundry detergents have nutritional value in the form of alkaline and phosphates as well as the microscopic organic particles from our body, which we leave on the clothes we wear and in our bath water. Experiments have shown that most plants grow and produce more when supplied with graywater than if they receive only potable water. However graywater should not be used for vegetable gardens, especially on plants that come into contact with soil, such as carrots and radishes. Graywater is acceptable for fruit trees, but should not be sprayed onto the fruit or trees themselves, due to bacteria and high alkaline level.

Some of the material I have read suggests that graywater should not be used on acid loving plants like hostas, because of high alkalinity from detergents. In my personal experiments of watering hostas with graywater, I have not produced any undesirable effects, although the soil in my area is somewhat acidic, which works in my favor. My final conclusion on using

Hosta   Fig. 1-1

graywater for hostas was that it's safer than the drought.

A severe drought in North Georgia gave me an opportunity to do some research with graywater and plants. I was surprised at the results. A friend of mine who bought some banana trees from a plant nursery in Florida gave me one. I planted it in mid-summer. At the end of summer I noticed the top leaves were considerably larger than the leaves which had been on the tree when it was growing at the nursery. When I checked the banana trees at my friend's house a few miles away, all the leaves were about the same size, from top to bottom. I have also noticed the oak trees in my yard produce an almost solid ground cover of acorns when they receive graywater about once a week.

Graywater Has Many Cost Effective and Environmental Benefits

- A graywater system can greatly extend the life of a septic system.

- Installing a graywater system may allow a drainfield which is suffering from hydraulic failure to recover, eliminating the need for expensive drainfield replacement.

- Graywater can replace much of the potable water currently being used for private landscape watering.

- Graywater is rich in nitrogen and phosphorus, which promote the growth of plants.

- Graywater can be used to provide plants with water during watering bans or restrictions.

- Using graywater for landscape plants reduces the amount of nitrogen-rich water flowing into lakes and streams from most waste treatment plants.

- Using graywater can reduce the burden on local utilities for both producing potable water and treating sewage.

- Graywater use can significantly reduce the cost of both water and sewage bills for the homeowner.

How Graywater Can Extend the Life of Septic System Drainfields

There are other water challenges for the homeowner besides the drought. In North Georgia as well as many other parts of the country, septic tanks and drainfields are buried in clay. Clay is a great filter until it becomes clogged with ingredients from our daily lives. **Home laundry is one of the greatest culprits of drainfield failure.** With each load of home laundry we add many gallons of water, about a quarter cup of salt and other detergent fillers and millions of micro-fibers which break loose from our clothes as they are being pounded by water and the mechanical scrubbing action of our washing machine. **A graywater system can greatly extend the life of a septic system by reducing the amount of water, detergents, organic material, and micro-fibers going into the drainfield.** Often a graywater system may reduce the amount of liquids flowing into a failed septic system enough to allow the drainfield to recover and function properly.

In fact, my own involvement with graywater was due to drainfield failure. A few years ago my panic-stricken wife called to inform me that we had sewage overflowing from the basement shower onto the floor. I immediately realized the seriousness of the situation when I found the yellow page ads for septic tank repair services were larger than the ads in the attorney section. After about 20 phone calls to the anytime day or night septic tank services, we found one company who would come out and pump our septic tank for a small fortune. The septic tank service people were kind enough to tell me that pumping out the tank was only a temporary fix. The semi-permanent fix would require replacing my drainfield at a cost of about $6,000 and destroying my entire front yard. Having spent most of my life on the sandy plains of North Carolina, drainfield failure was new to me.

At the time of my drainfield failure, I knew very little about graywater, but it seemed like a possible answer to my drainfield problem. With the power of the Internet at my fingertips, I expected to learn everything there was to know about graywater and find a source for any components needed to build a graywater system. The available information was limited and the needed components often did not exist. I had limited graywater knowledge, but with 25 years of engineering experience, I started building a graywater system. When completed, I had turned a $6,000 problem into a $1,000 solution, significantly reduced the amount of water going into my septic system and lowered my water bill.

Although my graywater system solved my immediate drainfield problem, I continued to research the cause of its failure, and investigate graywater systems further. One of the first things I learned was that septic systems in the piedmont regions of the southeastern part of the U.S. fail at an alarming rate. A properly installed septic system should provide the homeowner with about 20 to 30 years of trouble-free service, with normal maintenance. (Normal maintenance is having a qualified service company pump, clean and inspect the tank every 3 to 5 years). In regions with clay soil, many septic systems fail in less than 10 years. Some septic systems fail in as little as 1 to 5 years. With lot sizes becoming smaller in most metropolitan areas, there is minimal room to add an additional drainfield.

Like most people, I succumb to change out of necessity or to improve my standard of living. Growth in the number of graywater systems installed will first come out of necessity due to failing septic systems, therefore Appendix A of this manual is dedicated to septic systems and their failure mode. As research continues to improve graywater systems and potable water shortages become more extreme, graywater will someday become a common household word.

Public Sewage Systems can Benefit from Graywater

Public sewage systems have many of the same problems that private homeowners have with septic systems. **Many of the most difficult problems in treating public sewage are from detergents and cleaners.** Although nearly all ingredients in detergent are biodegradable, the process takes more time than most sewage treatment facilities can allow in their process. When the sewage treatment process is complete, the water still often contains detergent residue and organic material, which is pumped into lakes and streams. The organic-rich liquid is high in nitrogen which decomposes rapidly in lakes and streams, removing much of the oxygen from water. Nitrogen-rich liquid promotes rapid growth of algae and aquatic plants. When the high nitrogen level is depleted by plant growth, the aquatic plants die and start to decay. The decaying process deprives the water of oxygen. Excessive growth of aquatic plants is considered unhealthy for a proper ecosystem. Much research is being done to determine the long-term effects of nitrogen-rich water being pumped into fresh water reservoirs.

Widespread graywater use can greatly reduce the amount of liquids going

into waste treatment facilities. When graywater is not combined with sewage or black water, the level of cleaning agents and microscopic particles of organic material (nitrogen) is greatly reduced. This allows more settling time in the waste treatment facilities and reduces the amount of nitrogen flowing into lakes and streams. Ultimately, widespread use of graywater could reduce the need to enlarge or build new water and waste treatment facilities in growing metropolitan areas.

Evolution Of Graywater

After 30 years of research in California, graywater was found to be one of the few safe things to use for landscape watering. There has been no reported case of illness associated with its use. California passed a law in 1994, which allows private homeowners to use graywater throughout the state. Prior to 1994, it was illegal to install a graywater system in California, but they gave a tax break to homeowners who broke the law and installed a graywater system. New York has prohibited the use of graywater, based on the fear of contaminating the soil with organic material. By contrast, Georgia's Governor Sonny Perdue plans to improve the state's water shortage condition by using graywater both privately and commercially. Most states are doing some form of graywater research, while a few states are still overlooking the fact that a small but growing percentage of the population are installing graywater systems on their properties. The first step in enacting laws to govern the use of graywater is to educate lawmakers and the public on the possible benefits of its use.

And Its Future?

One day the use of graywater could be as commonplace again as it was before the advent of indoor plumbing. With bath and laundry water taking care of our landscape, we will save precious drinking water for ourselves.

The website listed below is a good source of information on graywater and water conservation. It will also direct you to other websites which are mostly maintained by universities or state agencies.

http://www.ces.ncsu.edu/depts/hort/consumer/hortinternet/water_conservation.html

SECTION 2

Graywater System Components

Since graywater has yet to enter the mainstream (no pun intended) of our society, few components have been developed for its use. Therefore it is necessary to use products which were originally intended for other purposes.

Throughout my career as an engineer, I have found that nearly all of my success has come from thinking outside the box. In the case of graywater, thinking outside the box required looking at a lot of different ways of doing things. Some worked out well and some didn't. For the sake of your time and my integrity, we will only cover the ones that have shown merit.

Conventional Near Surface Drainfield Cutaway View

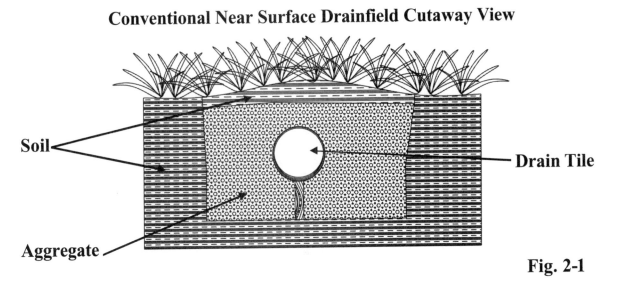

Soil

Drain Tile

Aggregate

Fig. 2-1

Near Surface Drainfield

Many state or local regulations for graywater systems require you to install a near surface drainfield. In the past such near surface drainfield designs were installed much like the ones used in a septic system drainfield. This type of system is quite expensive and offers little advantage to landscape watering. Installation of a conventional near surface drainfield system requires digging a wide trench, usually with a backhoe or other heavy equipment. Next, boards are placed vertically down the center of the trench. The boards are held in place by wooden stakes and checked for proper slope. Aggregate is then placed in the trench, to the top of the boards. Perforated drainpipe is then placed on top of the board and held in place by wire, to keep the drainpipe from floating up as aggregate is placed around the drainpipe. When the drainpipe is covered with aggregate, a layer of topsoil is slightly mounded over the trench, to allow for settling.

The expense of installing a conventional drainfield system is obvious, based on the equipment and labor involved. Other problems with this type of system may not be as obvious:

- Most of the water will pool along the bottom of the trench. If grass is planted over the drainfield, the aggregate and surrounding soil must be saturated before graywater will supply any surface roots like grass.

- Since the round perforated pipe is near the surface, it is subject to damage from riding lawn mowers or other equipment.

- This type of drainfield system will have a large impact on any existing landscape.

These problems were serious enough to warrant a search for better alternatives. Thinking outside the box led me to a product called AKWADRAIN™ (Fig. 2-2). AKWADRAIN, or strip drain, is a prefabricated plastic soil drain, designed for removing surface water and near surface ground water. The strip drain has two parts: (1) a core for collecting and moving water, and (2) a filter fabric cover to allow water to enter or exit the core while restraining soil particles that might clog the core. The standard strip drain is 6" wide, 1" thick and comes in 50' rolls.

Fig. 2-2

Conventional round perforated drainpipe has a very limited number of holes that would quickly become clogged if directly covered with soil. Since AKWADRAIN has a continuous cover of non-woven fabric, it can be buried in soil without being surrounded by aggregate.

Installation of a near surface drainfield using strip drain requires only digging a trench 3 to 4" wide with a power trencher which can be rented at most equipment rental locations. Depending on local or state requirements in your area, a trench should be dug 10 to 15" deep. Place the strip drain in the trench to fit against the side of the trench. Best performance is achieved when the strip drain has approximately 1 degree of slope or about 1/4" per foot. If the soil that was removed from the trench is loose and dry, it is acceptable to backfill the trench with the same soil. If the soil removed from the trench is either wet, lumpy, or clay the trench should be backfilled with sand to reduce settling.

Note: When backfilling with the same soil removed from the trench, be sure it is well compacted around the AKWADRAIN, or backfill with sand.

The strip drain method has less impact on landscaping and allows graywater to enter the soil near the surface, where it can be absorbed by grass or other plant roots.

The narrow profile of AKWADRAIN is less likely to be damaged by lawn mowers or other equipment moving over the drainfield area (Fig. 2-3).

Splicing rolls of strip drain can be done using AKWADRAIN's straight connectors or Tee connectors for branch drains. Adaptors are also available which allow strip drain to be connected to either corrugated pipe or smooth-wall plastic drain pipe (Fig. 2-4).

Graywater Near Surface Drainfield Cutaway

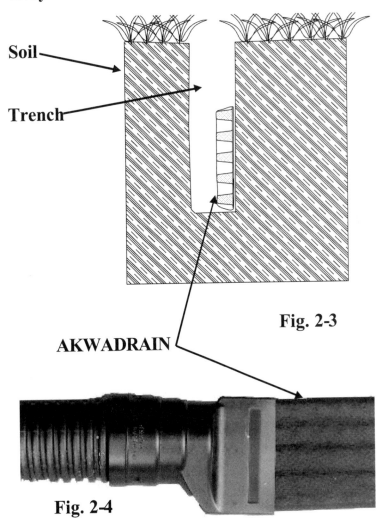

Soil

Trench

Fig. 2-3

AKWADRAIN

Fig. 2-4

The one drawback of AKWADRAIN is that it can eventually become clogged by roots of some plants. This condition does not usually present a problem under grass, or from most trees. AKWADRAIN can be covered with copper screen to prevent roots from growing into the inner core. Copper screen will not harm plants. The manufacturers of AKWADRAIN also carry a product called RootShield, to inhibit root growth. Additional information about these products can be found at, **http://www.americanwick.com**.

Surge Tanks

A primary component in a graywater system is the *surge tank*. As the name implies it receives rapid surges of graywater, while a pump or gravity empties graywater from the tank at a slower rate.

A surge tank is needed because graywater can flow from items like bathtubs and washing machines very rapidly. A top-loading washing machine can pump out about 15 gallons of water into the surge tank in less than a minute. Most graywater treatment systems or near surface drainfields cannot accept water at this rate. The capacity of a surge tank should be based on the largest capacity that will flow into the tank in a short period of time. A 30 gallon surge tank is adequate for home laundry. When showers and bathtubs are added to the graywater system, the surge tank should have a capacity of at least 50 gallons. Remember, there may be multiple sources flowing into a surge tank at the same time. Drain lines or pumps used to empty the surge tank should be set to start the outflow at a low water level from the surge tank. The surge tank should have a top opening large enough to place the connections, filter or, in some cases, a pump inside.

A *bag filter* on the inlet side of the surge tank is used to remove strings, hair and larger particles which would tend to clog pumps or drainfield lines. The *bag filter* should be made of materials which are not subject to rot or promote algae growth. No part of the filter should be subject to rust. The filter should be a screw-on type, to allow for easy filter replacement. The filter should not be too restrictive, as it is only used to catch larger particles, hair and strings. Having a filter with a very fine mesh would require replacement too frequently. Under normal conditions, the filter should be replaced about once per year, but should be checked more frequently during the first year to determine replacement intervals.

The surge tank in Fig. 2-5 is typically used in a graywater system built in a basement or garage. This tank is made of plastic and is easy to modify or add vent pipes, fill and drain lines. A Vent Pipe on top of the surge tank allows the tank to breathe. This will prevent backpressure from building up as the surge tank fills rapidly. It should be connected to one of the house vents which runs through the roof.

Surge Tank With Bag Filter

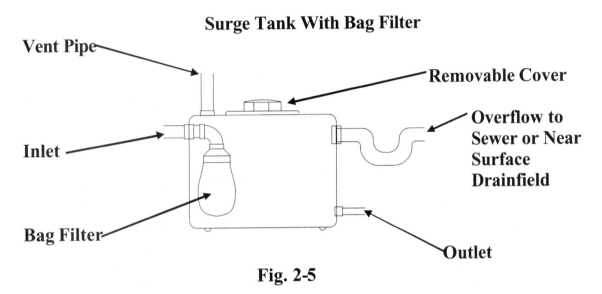

Fig. 2-5

Surge tanks may be used with a pump to move graywater into a near surface drainfield or to transfer graywater into a storage tank.

Fig. 2-6 is a photograph of a concrete distribution tank. This works well as a surge tank when buried just beneath the surface. It has 1 inlet and 5 outlet holes for connecting near surface drain lines. If there are 3 or more drain lines connected to this type of tank, it should remain trouble free without a bag filter.

Note: A baffle such as the one shown in Fig. 2-6 or screen filer can be installed to slow down the flow of liquid through the tank or catch hair and stings.

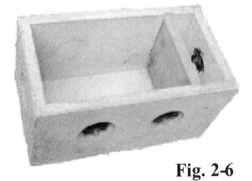

Fig. 2-6

Storage Tanks

In more elaborate graywater systems, a larger storage tank may be needed. There are several types of storage tanks that may be used for graywater. The size and style depend on the amount of treated graywater to be stored, and the best location for storage. We will cover several types of storage tanks and the installation methods.

Storage tanks can range from tall vertical tanks, which are normally placed in a basement or storage shed, to large underground tanks. Vertical storage tanks are normally selected by the size which will fit through an opening or doorway. For a doorway which is 3' wide, a 300 gallon tank is about the maximum size. Doorways with less than a full 3' in width will only allow for a 150 gallon tank, which is 23" in diameter. Multiple tanks may be desired to store a larger amount of treated graywater.

The cylinder tank, shown in Fig. 2-7 is available from **CHEM-TAINER™ Industries.**

To install a cylinder type of tank in an enclosed area, there are several modifications which must be made to the tank (Fig. 2-8). The top cover should be disassembled and sealed with a high quality silicon sealer.

Fig. 2-7

Cylinder tanks come with two bulkheads mounted for plumbing attachments. Whenever possible the overflow should be connected to allow discharge into a near surface drainfield (Fig. 2-9). Additional bulkheads may be installed for pumping graywater into the tank and for ventilation to the outside. More possible ways of using this type of tank will be discussed in Section 3 Graywater Systems.

Silicon Sealer

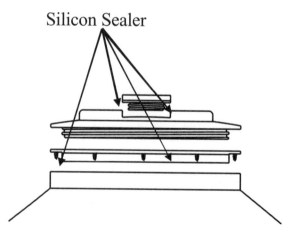

Fig. 2-8

Fig. 2-9 Modified Graywater Storage Tank

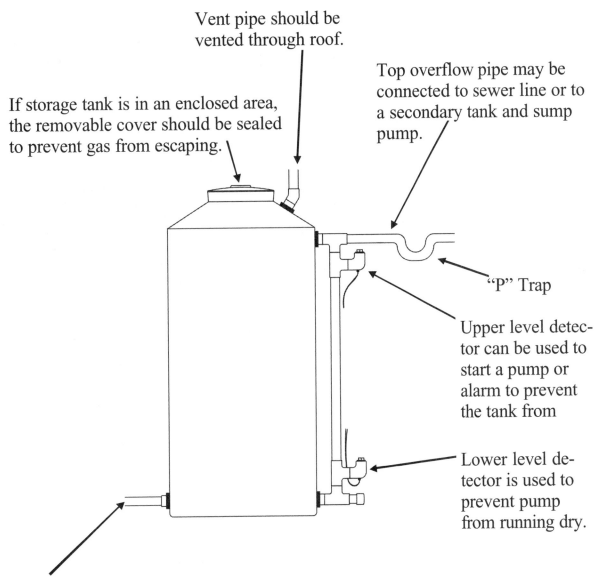

Vent pipe should be vented through roof.

Top overflow pipe may be connected to sewer line or to a secondary tank and sump pump.

If storage tank is in an enclosed area, the removable cover should be sealed to prevent gas from escaping.

"P" Trap

Upper level detector can be used to start a pump or alarm to prevent the tank from

Lower level detector is used to prevent pump from running dry.

Lower fill/drain port.
Using the same ports for drain and fill as well as level detection will cause pumps to short cycle or surge.

NOTE: If top overflow is connected to sewage drain, a "P" trap should be installed between the tank and sewage line to prevent sewer gas from entering storage tank.

Underground Storage Tank

Fig. 2-10

The concrete septic tank in Fig. 2-10 may be buried for bulk storage of treated graywater. Plastic septic tanks have thinner walls and are not suitable for any application in which the water will be removed from the tank. Because an empty tank can become buoyant, it is a good idea to place earth anchors 24 to 36" deep into the soil, underneath the tank. Use stainless steel cables to attach the tank to the earth anchors. A 1,000 gallon tank will have about 5,000 pounds of buoyancy when empty. Earth anchors and hold-down cable should be sized accordingly. Even a concrete tank like this one can float to the surface when empty, during heavy rains.

Earth Anchors

There are two types of earth anchors. My favorite design is called a "duck bill" (Fig. 2-11). It is driven into the ground with a steel rod. When the steel rod is removed and the cable is pulled tight, the anchor turns in the soil to lock into place. The other design of earth anchor uses an auger design, which screws into the soil (Fig. 2-12).

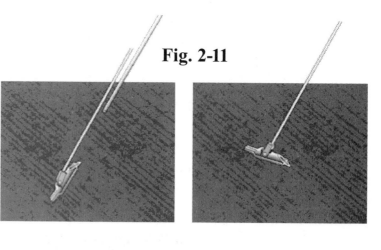

Fig. 2-11

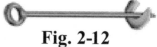

Fig. 2-12

Pumps

The most basic graywater system may not need a pump; however, adding a pump will allow you to move graywater uphill or into remote areas for plant watering. The simplest pump for graywater is a sump pump with float switch (Fig. 2-13). By placing a sump pump inside a surge tank, the float switch can automatically control the pump operation, empting the tank then shutting off the pump. Sump pumps can move an adequate volume of graywater if you are not pumping the graywater more than about 20' up, or about 100' horizontally.

Fig. 2-13

Lawn sprinkler pumps (Fig. 2-14) are a good choice for pumping graywater through filter systems and for pumping treated graywater into sprinkler systems. A water level monitoring system will need to be used to control the pump and prevent it from running dry.

Fig. 2-14

A standard shallow well pump and pressure tank (Fig. 2-15) can be used in a graywater system for manual watering of plants with treated graywater. This type of system can be purchased completely assembled with tank and pressure control switch.

Check-valves should always be used with pumps to prevent water from flowing back into the tank, after it is pumped out. Check-valves can be purchased at most builder supply outlets (Fig. 2-16).

Fig. 2-15

Flow

Fig. 2-16

Filters

Filters are an important part of a graywater system. The most basic type is a bag filter (Fig. 2-17). Bag filters are made of nylon mesh, which will not promote mildew or rot. The mesh is loose enough to allow easy flow of graywater and small organic particles, but should catch hair, strings and the occasional larger particles going down the drain. Bag filters are easily replaced by a screw-on or push-on adaptor, and should be replaced at least once per year.

Without a bag filter, strings, hair, and debris can become lodged in pumps or check-valves, which can eventually reduce their performance or even cause failure. Although normal replacement of bag filters should be once per year, each individual system is different and should be checked more often during the first year to determine if more frequent replacement is required.

Fig. 2-17

Sand Filter

Sand filters may be used in more elaborate systems, where treated graywater is to be stored for an extended period of time. Sand filters may also be used in systems utilizing small drip lines for individual plants, to prevent the drip valves from clogging with micro-fiber or lint. An ordinary swimming pool sand filter may be used to remove much of the organic material and micro-fiber (Fig. 2-18).

The sand filter in Fig. 2-18 is one of the more popular types. It consists of a molded polymeric tank, a top mounted control valve and a series of slotted tubes, called laterals (Fig. 2-19) near the bottom of the filter tank. The laterals fold out in all directions from a large vertical tube in the center of the tank. Sand is placed in the tank to the fill line, which covers the **Fig. 2-18** laterals. When the valve assembly is installed and hoses are assembled, graywater is pumped into the top of the filter tank. A spreader at the base of the valve assembly spreads water evenly over the top of the sand. The graywater is filtered as it flows through the sand and down into the lateral tubes. The filtered graywater then goes up the center tube and out the control valve assembly.

The sand filter control valve assembly can be set to backwash, for cleaning. In the backwash setting previously filtered graywater is pumped through the sand in the reverse direction and out the waste port of the valve. In normal mode, much of the organic materials and micro-fibers settle on or near the top surface of the sand. When the filter is backwashed,

Fig. 2-19

most of the organic materials removed by the filter will be washed out of the sand and through the waste port of the control valve. The filter's waste port should be connected to a near surface drainfield, where the soil bacteria will quickly break down the organic material. Approximately once per year the sand filter should be removed from the system for cleaning and sand replacement.

GRAVITY SAND FILTER

Some graywater systems have been developed which use a large sand-filled concrete septic tank for filtering graywater. The gravity sand filter requires very little maintenance and in some cases may not require a pump. This type of filter is normally constructed on site.

Gravity Sand Filter Construction

Most companies that manufacture concrete septic tanks can easily alter hole locations as the concrete tanks are being poured. This is the best time to have holes properly placed in the tank. Concrete tanks used for graywater have holes in different places than regular septic tanks (Fig. 2-20). A hole which will allow a 4" drain pipe must be placed in the end of the tank, as near the bottom as possible. This will allow filtered graywater to flow out of the tank. Next, a bulkhead or fitting is assembled through the end wall. After locating a proper site to bury the filter tank, excavation should be completed in accordance with the manufacturer's procedure. Prepare the bottom of the excavated hole, then place and level the tank. On the inside of the tank, connect an AKWADRAIN adaptor to the bottom bulkhead, then use about 25' of AKWADRAIN strip drain in a circular fashion in the bottom of the tank. Use sand to hold the strip drain in place. The strip drain should encircle the bottom of the tank, with the outer ring about 6" from the inside wall of the tank. Evenly space the remaining strip drain as it winds inward toward the tank center.

Once the strip drain is in place and covered with sand, continue filling the tank with sand until it is approximately 1' from the overflow drain port of the tank. Next install a pipe onto the inlet side of the tank and attach an AKWADRAIN adaptor to bring the bottom of the strip drain even with the surface of the sand. Install strip drain on the surface of the sand in the same manner as the bottom of the tank and cover with sand. Use approximately 50' of strip drain for the top layer. This will reduce any chance of clogging up with fiber and organic material.

The top outlet port of the gravity sand filter should be attached to a near surface drainfield. This will allow for overflow, if water flows into the filter more rapidly than it can flow through the system.

After sanitizing, the filtered graywater from a gravity sand filter such as the one in Fig. 2-20 may be used for surface watering or stored in an underground or an above-ground reservoir for later use.

Gravity Sand Filter Side View

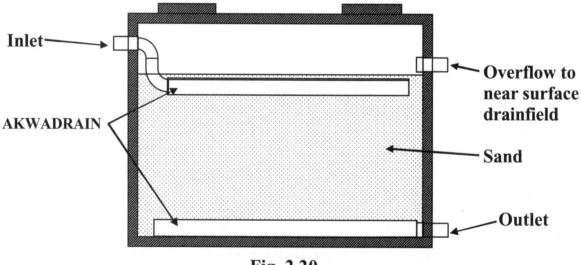

Fig. 2-20

NOTE: Positive ventilation should always be provided into any tank when a worker is inside.

Applied Process Technology
Conroe, Texas
Centra-flo™ Gravity Sand Filter

Fig. 2-21

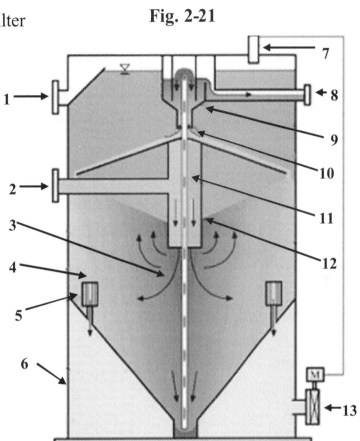

1. Over Flow
2. Filter Influent
3. Course Media
4. Fine Media
5. Filtrate Nozzles
6. Filtrate Chamber
7. Level Controller
8. Filter Reject
9. Washbox
10. Counter-Current Washer
11. Airlift
12. Central Feed Chamber
13. Actuated Valve

The Centra-flo™ Gravity Sand Filter (Fig. 2-21) was designed for commercial applications where large amounts of water are to be filtered. Sand in this system is continually cleansed, so shutdown for backwashing is not required. Filtered water from this type of system is often sanitized by ultra violet light then pumped into holding ponds for irrigation. A filter system like this is used by the city of Winder, GA, where the filtered and sanitized water is used for irrigation of a local golf course. Similar systems could be built to provide a cost effective way for landscape watering of many office buildings, hotels and resorts.

After graywater is filtered by a sand filter system, it still contains nitrogen and phosphorus, making it ideal for watering grass or landscape plants. If the filtered and treated water is stored in holding ponds, it should have a system installed for adding oxygen back into the water. Oxygen levels are depleted as nitrogen in the water decays.

Sanitizers

As with water stored in a swimming pool, graywater must be sanitized to prevent bacteria and algae from growing. The main difference between graywater and water in a swimming pool is that we have little control of the pH range in graywater. Chlorine is an effective sanitizer as long as the pH range is between 7.2 and 7.6. Soap and detergents can change the pH range enough to render chlorine ineffective.

Bromine is an effective sanitizer over a much greater pH range than chlorine. Bromine is also less harmful to plants than chlorine. As with water in a swimming pool, bromine can be added by circulating the water through a canister filled with bromine tablets. The canister in Fig. 2-22 has an adjustment control to set the amount of bromine being added to the water.

Fig. 2-22

The bromine canister in Fig. 2-23 is the type which floats. A string attached to the top will allow you to lower this type of bromine feeder down into a storage tank, then remove it to add bromine once-a-month.

Fig. 2-23

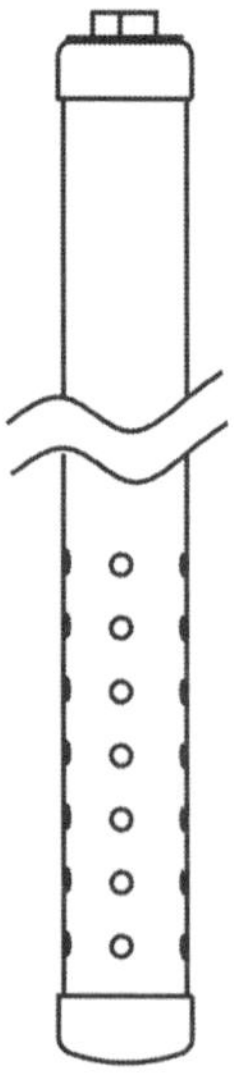

Fig. 2-24

A bromine canister for buried graywater holding tanks may be built from a 4" PVC pipe with holes drilled through the sides (Fig 2-24). The bottom has a glue-on end cap. The top cap is removable for adding bromine.

(About 2 lb of bromine should be added to the canister each month.)

Ozone Generators

Ozone generators kill germs without chemicals. Ultra-violet light or corona generators are used to convert oxygen into ozone, which is injected into the water in the form of tiny bubbles. As the ozone molecules come into contact with organic matter, they convert back into oxygen as they break up the organic molecules. This process is effective in killing bacteria, viruses, molds, mildews and eliminates spores, yeast and fungus. Ozone generators have been used in Europe for treatment of swimming pools for more than 50 years. Today this method of sanitizing swimming pools and municipal water is gaining popularity in the US. Ozone is effective over the entire pH range. In some areas of the country researchers are evaluating the use of ozone generators for treating sewage.

Valves

Key graywater components like pumps and filters should have shutoff valves installed to allow these components to be removed for repair or replacement. The best type of valve to use is a ball valve (Fig. 2-25). Ball-valves cause little or no turbulence as graywater flows through the open valve. Valves which have internal restrictions when open require more work for pumps and may catch strings or hair which could eventually cause the valve to fail.

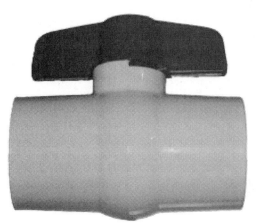

Fig. 2-25

Unions

A union (Fig. 2-26) is a device which allows pipes to be coupled together, and disassembled for easy removal of filters which may need occasional cleaning.

Fig. 2-26

Pipe

Some states require special pipe to be used in graywater systems. The special pipe is colored purple, has a purple stripe or, in most cases a stripe of purple tape along the pipe is acceptable. The purple stripe is helpful in allowing easy identification of graywater pipes, when mixed with other drainpipes. Most home improvement stores sell purple PVC pipe cleaner for cleaning joints prior to gluing. The purple cleaner can be used to paint a permanent stripe on the pipe either before or after installation.

Fluid Level Detectors

Where pumps are used, it is often necessary to monitor graywater levels to prevent the pump from running dry. Fig. 2-27 is a level detector which can be mounted onto a 2" pipe which connects the lower fill/drain port to an upper fill/drain port, to monitor graywater level. Switches like this are normally connected to a controller which controls power to a pump. In some cases there is a requirement to have the pump

Fig. 2-27

turn on when the tank is full to prevent the tank from overflowing. At this time controllers must be custom built for each individual system into which it is being installed. We are currently working on a more universal controller which could be installed, then programmed to the needs of the system.

Bulkheads

Bulkheads like the one in Fig. 2-28 are mounted in plastic tanks to adapt plumbing.

Fig. 2-28

Poly Tubing

Fig. 2-30

Fig. 2-29

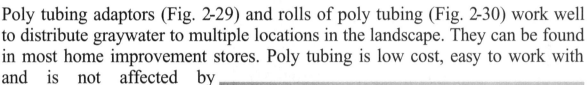

Poly tubing adaptors (Fig. 2-29) and rolls of poly tubing (Fig. 2-30) work well to distribute graywater to multiple locations in the landscape. They can be found in most home improvement stores. Poly tubing is low cost, easy to work with and is not affected by freezing.

Timer

I have been fairly successful in using off-the-shelf timers such as the one in Fig. 2-31. This type of timer can be used to empty a tank daily and can be programmed to control valves to target different zones, so the graywater is not always going to the same plants. **Fig. 2-31**

As new components and methods are tested and proven to work well in graywater systems, we will provide information about these developments. Go to **http://www.graywaterresource.com** for future developments and components.

SECTION 3

Graywater Systems

Graywater systems can be as simple as a small surge tank and near surface drainfield, all the way up to multiple tanks, pumps, filtering systems and controller to automatically water plants. The ideal time to start a graywater system is during the development of a new home. Even if a homeowner has no immediate plans of installing a graywater system, provision should be made to keep graywater from mixing with sewage until it exits the home. This can be accomplished by connecting all sewage or black water fixtures to a single main drain. These fixtures include toilets, urinals, bidets, dishwashers and any area where food is prepared. Typically this would be a 4" drain line. A separate drain line is installed to connect the bathtubs, showers, whirlpools, bathroom sinks and laundry. A 2" drain will accommodate most graywater designs. A three-way valve should be installed to divert laundry water into the sewage lines if diapers are to be laundered. The graywater drain and sewage drain should be joined at a single point, either inside or just outside the home. This will allow the homeowner to easily split the system at a later date and attach to a surge or storage tank and near surface drainfield.

Adding a graywater system to an existing home is not difficult, although it does require some knowledge of basic plumbing skills. If you are lacking in these skills your local home improvement center is an excellent source of books and information to help you get started.

Most homes built during the past 50 years have either ABS or PVC (plastic) drain lines. These are easy to work with and make modifications to. Modifying a drain line to divert it to a graywater system usually requires you to remove a short section of pipe, redirect the flow of graywater and seal off the sewage side of the drain (Fig. 3-1 and Fig 3-2).

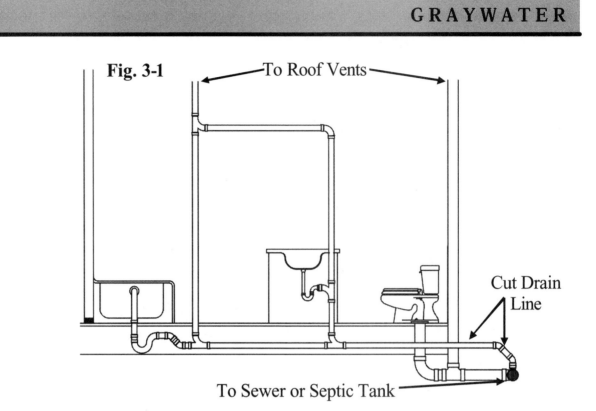

Fig. 3-1

To Roof Vents

Cut Drain Line

To Sewer or Septic Tank

Fig. 3-1 is an illustration of a typical drainage system. To modify for attaching a graywater system, cut out a section of drain pipe near the main drain line. As shown in Fig. 3-2, add an end cap or plug to seal off the sewer line. Add a coupling and new pipe to extend a drain line into the graywater system.

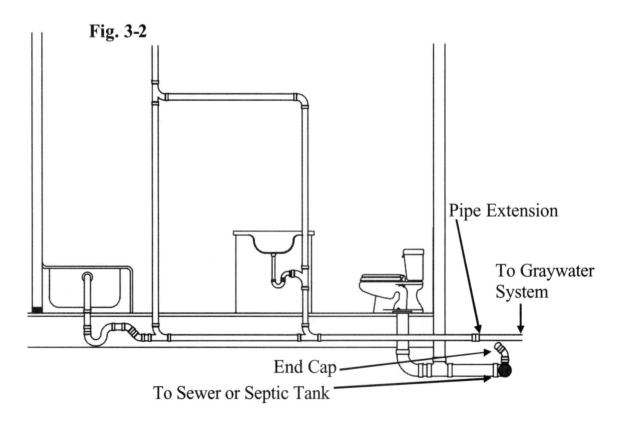

Fig. 3-2

Pipe Extension

To Graywater System

End Cap

To Sewer or Septic Tank

BUILDING A GRAYWATER SYSTEM

Putting graywater components together into a complete system may require a little imagination. The type of system you install will depend primarily on your objective. Whether the need is for extending the life of a septic system or meeting the watering needs of landscaping or lawn, we will give several examples and illustrations of various systems to assist in coming up with your own ideas of the system best suited to your situation.

The first step is to contact your state or local agencies to determine if there are any graywater requirements in your area. Typically the same agency which handles septic system installation inspections will also have information about any state or local graywater requirements. Many states have little or no laws governing the installation of a graywater system. Some states which do have graywater regulations, have documents which can be downloaded from the Internet.

If installing your graywater system requires any form of digging or trenching, you will first need to have your underground utilities marked. Most areas have a single number to call which will set the process in motion for all the utility companies in your neighborhood. The utility company will place small flags and paint stripes on your lawn, indicating buried cables or gas line. This is normally a free service and typically takes about 2 to 5 working days to complete. Any one of your utility companies should be able to give you the phone number for this service.

Any plumbing changes or additions for a graywater system should meet local and state codes and practices. If you are unsure of your local plumbing codes, it is advisable to seek the advice of a professional plumber.

Some other considerations for graywater systems are the location of septic tank and drainfield, as well as private water well. Any near surface drainfield lines should maintain the same distance requirements from water wells as if they were sewage drainfield lines. Each state has different distance requirements from water wells to septic tanks and drainfields.

Fig. 3-3 shows an overhead view of a typical 1 acre lot with a private water well and septic system. (Note: Surge tank and AKWADRAIN added for graywater system.) A similar drawing of your property can usually be obtained from your county health department or the local agency which handles permits for wells and septic systems.

Overhead View of Lot With Well, Septic System and Graywater System

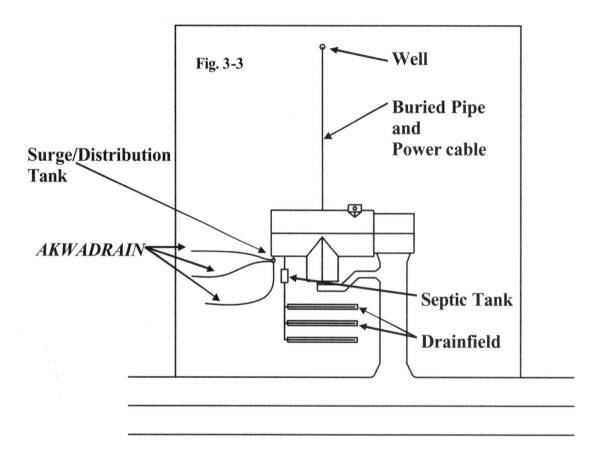

Deciding on the type of graywater system to install should be based on the objectives you wish to accomplish. The following system configurations are examples which may be used for ideas and may be altered, or components from one type of system, in some cases, may be blended with components from other systems.

Fig. 3-4 illustrates a basic graywater system to relieve hydraulic loading on a septic system and provide near surface ground water for landscape plants or trees. This type of system is very basic, requiring only a surge/distribution tank, filter and gravity-fed near surface drainfield.

Installing a graywater system in a home with a basement or crawl space is much easier than in a home built on a concrete slab. If the objective is to reduce hydraulic loading on a septic system, the return on investment may be well worth the effort, even on a concrete slab. A simple system like the one above can reduce hydraulic loading on the average septic system by 20 to 30%. The system in Fig. 3-4 has a concrete distribution/surge tank buried just beneath the soil surface.
Note: See Section 2 on graywater components for more information on surge tanks and near surface drainfields.

Side View of House on Concrete Slab with Graywater System

Fig. 3-4

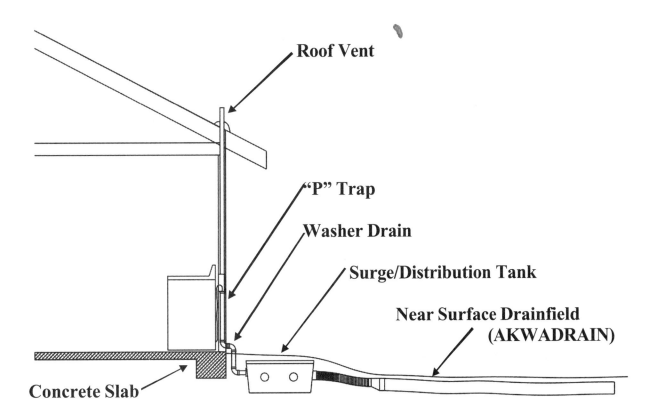

The system shown in Fig. 3-5 can be altered in several ways. The drain line may be run farther away from the house and the surge/distribution tank may be buried in an area where it is surrounded by landscape plants. The distribution tank has several drain ports which will allow near surface drain lines to be run out in different directions.

Fig. 3-5   **Top View**

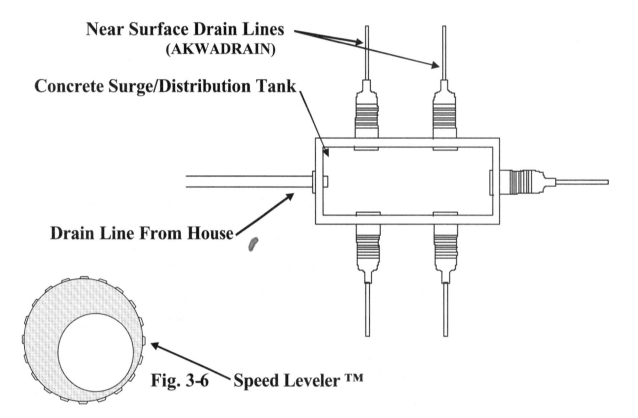

Near Surface Drain Lines
(AKWADRAIN)

Concrete Surge/Distribution Tank

Drain Line From House

Fig. 3-6 Speed Leveler ™

When installing a distribution tank with multiple drain lines, it is important to have water flowing out into each drain line at the same rate. This is accomplished by using a special leveling insert (available from most tank suppliers) which snaps into each 4" drain line (Fig. 3-6). Once the tank is in place, fill the distribution tank with water until it starts to flow out through the smaller hole in the Speed Leveler ™ inserts, then adjust each insert until water flows equally into each drain line.

Installation of a basic underground graywater system

1. Start by digging a hole approximately 8" larger than the surge/distribution tank.

2. Next pour a 3 to 4" concrete base in the bottom of the hole. This will prevent the tank from settling and becoming uneven (Fig. 3-7).

Fig. 3-7

Fig. 3-8

3. Place the surge tank onto concrete base (Fig. 3-8).

4. Dig trenches to receive drain lines and AKWAD-RAIN.

5. Install 4" drain lines into the ports which will be connected to AKWADRAIN lines.

6. Attach adapters and AKWADRAIN (Fig. 3-9).

Fig. 3-9

Fig. 3-10 is the surge tank with four drain lines with speed levelers and a concrete baffle installed.

A "T" with a screw out plug was installed on the inlet line to allow easy inspection for standing water in the system or to allow copper sulfate to be poured into the system to prevent roots from plugging the AKWADRAIN lines.

Fig. 3-10

Note: See warning on copper sulfate in Appendix A, pg. 68.

When the concrete cover is installed and the hole is backfilled, nothing is visible but the top of the PVC plug.

The concrete baffle prevents graywater from flowing rapidly from the inlet line to the adjacent drainfield outlet line.

In Fig. 3-11 each of the Speed Levelers are adjusted so that graywater will start to flow out of all drain lines at the same water level.

Below, (Fig. 3-12 and 3-13) AKWADRAIN is placed in trenches, checked for proper slope then backfilled.

After AKWADRAIN is properly placed in trenches, the soil should be well compacted around it. If the soil removed from the trench is not loose enough to compact, then sand should be used for backfilling to prevent settling.

Fig. 3-11

Fig. 3-12

Fig. 3-13

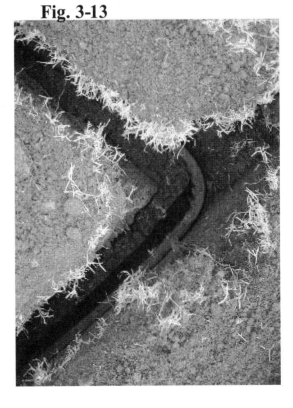

The near surface drainfield shown in Fig. 3-5 through Fig. 3-13, should have about 200 linear feet of near surface drain line if installed in clay soil. Sandy loam soil only needs about 150 linear feet. Care should be taken to maintain a 1 degree slope on all the drain lines. If you are installing a near surface drainfield on a steeper slope, the drain lines may be run diagonally or zigzag to reduce the rate of decline.

Reminder: When installing a surge/distribution tank with three or more output drain lines going into a near surface drainfield, it may not be necessary to have a bag or screen filter inside the tank. This type of system is virtually maintenance free.

Adding a Pump to the Basic Graywater System

The addition of a sump pump and float switch in a surge/distribution tank will allow plants in remote locations to be supplied with graywater. The surge tank should still have a gravity-fed near surface drainfield to receive any overflow, or to operate in the event of power or pump failure. This basic design can be taken a step further by installing a timer switch to control the sump pump. The timer switch will allow the pump to empty the surge tank one day and simply drain out into the near surface drainfield the next day. Power can be disconnected to the sump pump during winter months when plants use very little water.
Note: Whenever any pump is installed into a graywater system, you should always install a bag filter or screen filter, to prevent strings and hair from causing pump failure.

One way to distribute graywater to multiple locations is to build a manifold for attaching poly tubing inside the surge/distribution tank. The continual injection of warm water into the tank will keep it from freezing in winter. The manifold can be made from off-the-shelf PVC pipe fittings, or to save space and money on pipe fittings, I drill holes into a short 2" PVC pipe, then use a 1/2" NPT tap to thread the holes. Next, 1/2" poly tube adaptors can be screwed directly into the PVC pipe. Fig. 3-14 shows a manifold with 10-1/2" poly tubing adaptors installed. The poly tubing can then be bundled together and run through one of the drain ports in the side of the surge/distribution tank. It is a good idea to run the poly tubing inside a few feet of 4" drain pipe (Fig. 3-14 and 3-15). Polyurethane foam sealer does a good job of sealing around the poly tubing to prevent graywater from running out of the tank and prevent surface water from running into the tank.

Manifold and Sump Pump

Out to Near Surface Drainfield

Inlet

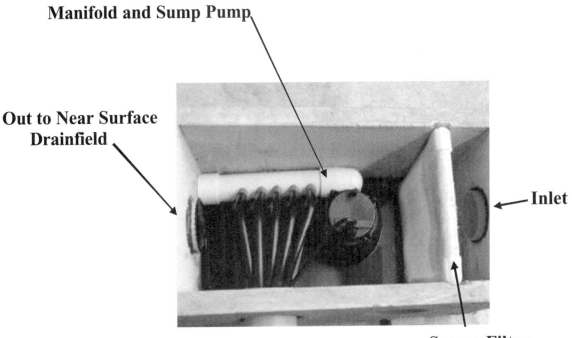

Screen Filter

Fig. 3-14

Note: Fig. 3-15 is for illustration purposes only; a larger surge/distribution tank should be used when installing a sump pump.

4" pipe to strip drain adaptor.

Fig. 3-15

Since poly tubing is not affected by freezing, it can be buried in a shallow trench or routed along the soil surface. When poly tubing is left on the surface it can be held in place by wire stakes and covered with mulch.

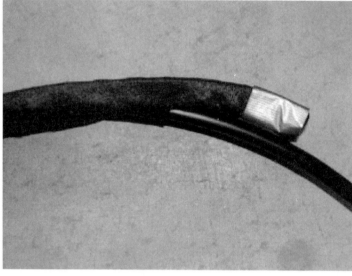

Fig. 3-16

Short sections of strip drain can be buried near plants or trees needing to be watered. Strip drain should be prepped by peeling back the outer cover on each end, cut off about 2" of the inner core and fold the outer cover over the end, then use duct tape to hold the cover in place. Cut a short slit into the outer cover of the strip drain and insert the end of the poly tubing, as shown in Fig. 3-16.

Planter

Planters like the one shown in Fig. 3-17 can be installed in public and office buildings, as well as private residences. Graywater from lavatory sinks may be used to establish nearly maintenance-free planters. If more water is pumped into the planter than needed, the excess will flow out the bottom drain to a near surface drainfield.

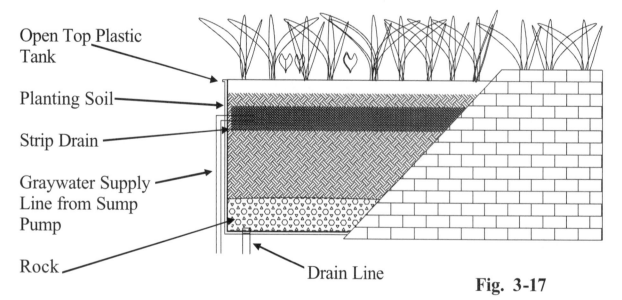

Open Top Plastic Tank

Planting Soil

Strip Drain

Graywater Supply Line from Sump Pump

Rock

Drain Line

Fig. 3-17

Irrigating With Graywater

Up to this point the graywater systems described in Section 3 were designed primarily for sub-terrain irrigation, which is by far the most efficient use of water. Although graywater is better suited for sub-terrain irrigation, it is not always practical for watering lawns, where water should be spread over a large area near the surface. Graywater which is dispensed above the ground by either drip irrigation or through sprinklers may come into contact with people or animals. Therefore it should be sanitized to kill bacteria and viruses (this is discussed in Section 2 on graywater components). Graywater should also undergo filtering to remove hair, strings and fibers, to prevent sprinklers from becoming clogged.

Designing a graywater system for above-ground irrigation is a bit more complex than a basic near surface drainfield system, but it can be done by the average do-it-yourselfer.

Some types of graywater treatment systems can be built inside a basement. The one shown in Fig. 3-18 requires only about 20 square feet of floor space.

Fig. 3-18

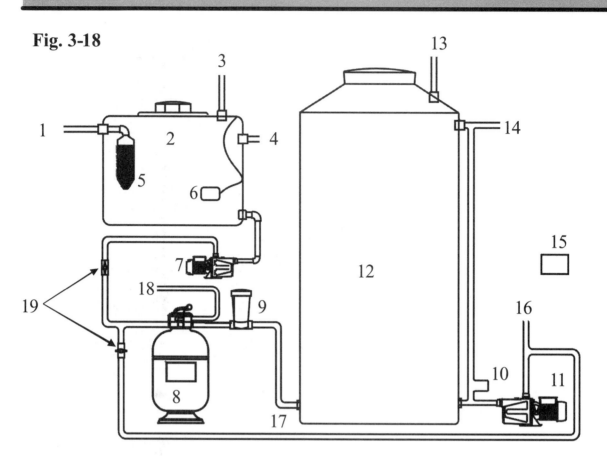

1. Graywater inlet from plumbing
2. Surge Tank
3. Vent (may be connected to plumbing vent)
4. Tank overflow connected to Sewage or Near Surface Drainfield
5. Bag Filter
6. Float Switch for Transfer Pump
7. Transfer Pump
8. Sand Filter
9. Bromine Canister
10. Water Level Detector (prevents pump from running with no water)
11. Irrigation Pump
12. Storage Tank
13. Vent (may be connected to plumbing vent)
14. Tank overflow connected to Sewage or Near Surface Drainfield
15. Timer to Control Pump and Sprinkler Valves
16. Outlet to Sprinkler Valves
17. Backwash Pipe
18. Waste from Sand Filter (connected to Near Surface Drainfield)
19. Backwash valves

Fig. 3-19

Surge Tank

Storage Tank

Transfer Pump

Bromine Canister

Sand Filter

Irrigation Pump

Washing Machine
Drip Pan

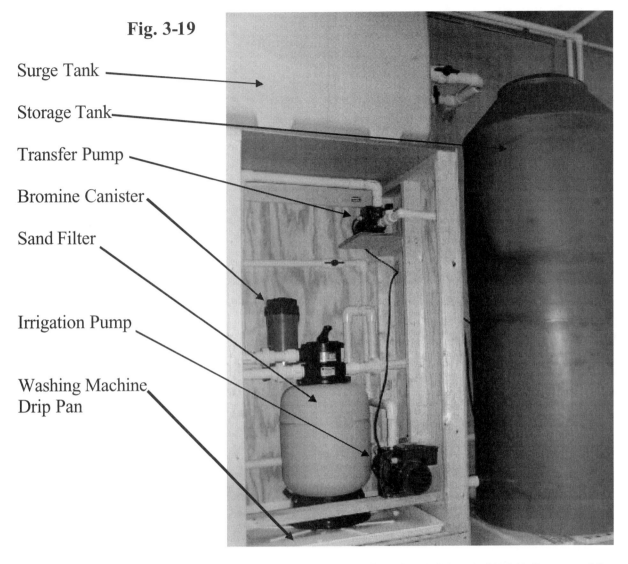

Fig. 3-19 is a photograph of the system drawing in Fig. 3-18. A 2'X4' frame with plywood sides was built to house the graywater components. The surge tank sits on top, this allows the graywater to flow down through the sand filter and bromine canister until the storage tank is nearly full. Although not shown in the drawing in Fig. 3-18, valves were installed to allow different parts of the system to be isolated or removed. A washing machine drip pan was placed in the bottom to catch any leaks, if they occur.

A graywater system of this type requires some maintenance:

- Once-a-week   Back wash Sand Filter
- Once-a-month   Add Bromine to canister
- Once-a-year   Replace Bag Filter and sand in Sand Filter

In addition to the transfer and irrigation pumps shown in the system in Fig. 3-18 and Fig. 3-19, a shallow well pump and pressure tank can be attached. The treated graywater from this type of pump may be used for hand watering individual plants.

Underground Graywater System

A virtually maintenance-free graywater system can be achieved by using some of the same components and concepts as a private septic system. This type of system offers better filtration of graywater and much more storage capacity for treated graywater.

If graywater is to be used for lawn watering, a system with a large reservoir is needed. The average household will not generate enough graywater on a daily basis to sustain most lawns. The ideal graywater system for watering lawns is large enough to store water during periods of ample rainfall, then stored graywater can be used for lawn irrigation during droughts. In some cases you may generate enough graywater to maintain your lawn as long as you have enough storage capacity to hold the graywater for several days, then use enough treated graywater to saturate the soil for a couple of inches.

Another way of reducing the amount of water needed for your lawn is to plant more drought tolerant grass like zoysia.

Fig. 3-20   **Underground Graywater Treatment System**

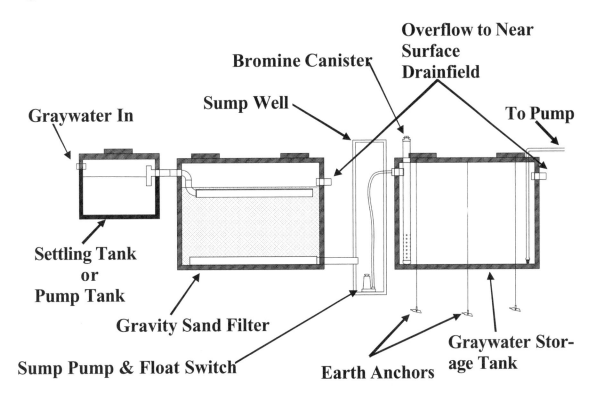

Fig. 3-20 illustrates an underground graywater system, made up of 3 concrete tanks. The first tank in the system is a settling and surge tank where some of the fibers and organic material have time to settle out before flowing into the sand filter. This tank is much like a traditional septic tank but does not need to be as large since there are almost no solids flowing into it.

Graywater flows out of the settling tank into the sand filter, where gravity and sand work together to clean and filter the water. The sand filter is made from a modified concrete septic tank. (Section 2 on Graywater Components) Bacteria in the sand filter works to break down the organic material from the graywater.

Filtered graywater flows out of the sand filter into a sump pit, which can be made from a section of 16" drain tile placed vertically near the end of the sand filter. The sump pump is used to transfer filtered graywater into the holding tank.

The storage tank is a concrete septic tank with a couple of modifications. The modifications are made to allow a 4" PVC pipe to be inserted through the top, to insert a bromine canister.

Additional holding tanks may be incorporated into an underground graywater treatment system to increase the amount of storage capacity.

A near surface drainfield should be installed for the Gravity Sand Filter and the Graywater Storage Tank. These will allow overflow in the event of graywater flowing into the Gravity Sand Filter more rapidly than it can flow through the filter or in the event of Sump Pump failure. Providing an overflow from the graywater storage tank will allow the system to remain maintenance free during winter months when no graywater is being used for irrigation.

Graywater from a properly built gravity sand filter system like the one shown in Fig. 3-20 should be almost completely clear and have virtually no odor. Treated graywater from this type of system should be suitable for toilet flushing and plant watering both above ground or below. The gravity filtering method is preferable to a pool type sand filter. Because graywater flows through the filter naturally, instead of being forced through by a pump, there is more surface area for the sand to collect organic particles, and bacteria has more time to break down the organic particles into water and gas.

Very little maintenance is required for a gravity sand filter, only adding bromine about once per month and ensuring proper operation of the pumps.

In Conclusion

In order for the use of graywater to make a positive impact on future water shortages, state and local governments need to enact legislation that will at least define their stand on the use of graywater. Private citizens need to encourage their elected officials to learn about graywater and the water-saving benefits.

Homebuilders should be encouraged to establish water-wise plumbing in new homes, that would allow easy hookup of a graywater system. The cost of adding this extra plumbing would have very little impact on the total cost of a new home. As water shortages become worse and the cost of both water and sewage treatment continue to rise, the benefits could be enormous over the life of a home.

Whether you need to relieve the stress on your septic system's drainfield or you desire a cost-effective means of watering your landscape, a graywater system may be a viable choice for you.

I invite you to share your graywater success stories and questions by contacting me through our website: **http://www.graywaterresource.com**

APPENDIX A

Septic System Failure: Its Prevention and Recovery

Septic system failure can be one of the most troublesome problems facing a homeowner today. Replacing an existing drainfield, or adding to one can be an expensive endeavor. In some cases there is an enormous amount of damage to property if sewage backs up and flows onto finished flooring or carpet. Drainfields are often placed in front of homes where landscaping can be completely destroyed by heavy equipment and digging. In many cases it can require a few years for the soil to settle properly and grass or groundcover to return to normal.

There is seldom enough space on most newer home sites for more than two drainfields. Most areas require lot sizes or building sites to have ample space for an additional drainfield, should (when) the first one fails. The question that many homeowners have is "If the first drainfield failed after only a few years, why should I expect the next one to last longer?"

To get to the root of drainfield problems we must look at the soil. In North Georgia we have what many people around the country refer to as "Red Georgia Clay". Those of us who suffer drainfield problems or just try to dig a hole for plants usually refer to it as "^&# %#! *^#*". The same properties that make clay useful for things like flower pots, brick and landfill covers, make it difficult for some plants and drainfields. The clay particles are extremely small compared to soils of many regions of the country, because they are the product of erosion from very hard rock like granite and gneiss. The red color comes primarily from oxidation of iron oxides (rust) in the soil.

The small size of clay particles leave very little space for soil pores or oxygen between soil particles. The more tightly compacted soil reduces movement of both oxygen and water through soil. The process of iron oxidation in soil reduces the amount of available oxygen, increases the acidic level and further breaks down soil components into even smaller particles. All of this reduces the efficiency of normal bacterial action for a properly working drainfield.

By definition clay is a soil particle <0.002 mm diameter. Silt particles are from 0.002 to 0.05 mm diameter and sand has a diameter of 0.05 to 2 mm. All this is important in the fact that for a drainfield to work properly it needs several things. One of the most important things in a properly working drainfield is oxygen. Oxygen is required to sustain life for the most active and beneficial bacteria in the soil, commonly known as aerobic bacteria. Bacteria such as protozoa, molds and fungi are in soil by the billions, working to break down organic particles into molecule size components that plants can absorb through the roots and process for growth and oxygen production. Fresh water is also important for keeping a drainfield working properly. As fresh water flows through the soil it carries nutrients, bacteria and oxygen deeper into the soil, as well as helping to dilute the effluent liquid flowing into drainfields.

Fig. A-1   **Relative size of soil particles:**

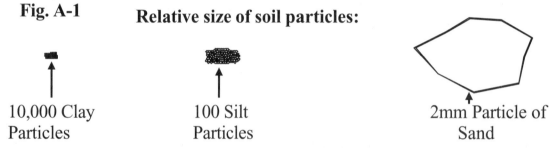

10,000 Clay Particles   100 Silt Particles   2mm Particle of Sand

Clay can sometimes swell when it remains saturated for an extended period of time, virtually sealing off its ability to absorb or percolate water through it. When this happens, the soil may never recover to the point where it can be a useful drainfield again.

The top 12 to 18 inches of soil are the most effective in sanitizing and treating effluent liquid. Earth worms, nematodes and bacteria all live in harmony near the surface to enrich the soil and breakdown organic particles. Most plant roots are also in the areas near the surface because that is where the nutrients are. Solar and wind evaporation are much more effective near the soil surface.

With all that said, most areas require drainfields to be buried 24 to 36 inches below the surface. In good quality soil like loam, which is a mixture of many soil sizes, the 36 inch depth will usually work quite well. Fresh water from the surface, bacteria and oxygen can travel through the top 12 or so inches of soil, where it reaches the aggregate surrounding drain pipes. Water can flow easily through the aggregate to carry beneficial bacteria and oxygen to lower portions of the drainfield and promote the breakdown of organic particles in the effluent liquid.

However, fresh water and oxygen cannot easily penetrate densely packed soil. Clay soils are further compacted by lawn mowing equipment, foot traffic and even rain. We further compound all these problems with things like laundry detergents which aid in filling small pores and further reducing liquid absorption into the soil.

Ingredients in detergent called surfactants act like magnets to attach themselves to dirt particles and keep them suspended in water. Almost everything we like about our laundry detergents have a negative effect in a septic system. Laundry detergent's primary function is to remove soil from clothing and keep it from reattaching during the wash cycle. While the washing machine's agitation and detergents do a good job of cleaning, they break loose millions of micro-fibers from fabrics. Surfactants continue to keep soil particles and micro-fibers suspended in the septic tank. Since the suspended particles, micro-fibers and organic matter often neither rise to the surface or sink to the bottom of the septic tank, they easily flow into the drainfield. Although surfactants are biodegradable, the breakdown process occurs very slowly in the drainfield, due to the lack of oxygen, reduced temperature and a relatively low amount of aerobic bacteria.

Laundry detergents also contain active ingredients, such as enzymes. **Enzymes are large, complex molecules that living cells make to carry out chemical reactions,** such as breaking down proteins like grass or blood stains. These molecules mix well with water and often remain suspended until they flow through the septic tank and into the drainfield.

Under ideal conditions, wastewater and sewage should have about a week in the septic tank to separate into different layers. With several loads of laundry and other normal household use, more than 50% of the septic tank's liquid can be replaced in a single day. With an excessive amount of water flowing into the septic tank in a short period of time, the amount of suspended particles flowing out of the septic tank and into the drainfield is greatly increased.

Poor soil quality for liquid absorption, compounded with detergents and organic particles, often create an environment that can greatly reduce the life of a septic system.

Septic Systems

To understand why septic systems fail, it is helpful to have some basic knowledge of their history and how they work.

The first septic tank was invented in 1860 by Louis M. Mouras of Vosoul, France. In English terms it was called the Mouras Automatic Scavenger. The earliest tanks were very large and designed to treat wastewater for entire communities. This initial treatment concept consisted of removing solids before the effluent liquid was discharged into local streams or rivers. Donald Cameron of Exeter, England gave the septic tank its name in 1895, when he installed a covered 53,000 gallon tank for anaerobic purification of sewage.

Leslie C. Frank and C.P. Rhymus with the U.S. Public Health Service conducted a study on the use of the septic tank and drainfield for private residence in 1919. Because the development was done by a government agency, there were no patent or royalty restrictions. This allowed basic septic systems or private waste treatment systems to be adopted on a wide-scale basis for single family residences. Although the septic system design has gone through many changes during the 20th Century, the basic principles of operation have not changed.

Many of the private septic systems installed in the U.S. were installed with the idea that they would be temporary until public sewage was installed. Because they were thought of as temporary, not much thought was given to longevity. Today we realize that in most areas of the country public sewage will probably never be installed, so the septic system is a permanent fixture.

Fig. A-2 shows a basic septic tank and drainfield.

Fig. A-2

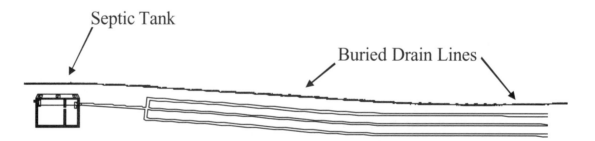

Septic Tank

Buried Drain Lines

Conceptually, septic systems are amazingly efficient. The septic tank is an ingenious product that has served the U.S. homeowner well for nearly a century. The basic concept is that waste and water are carried by gravity into a large holding tank, or septic tank. In the septic tank (Fig. A-3), sewage should have about a week to start to decompose and separate. Solids form a layer on the bottom of the tank, called the **sludge layer**. Paper, grease and lighter particles form a layer on the surface called the **scum layer.** The mostly liquid layer between the **sludge layer** and the **scum layer** is called the **effluent**. Baffles or a **sanitary "T"** inside the septic tank prevent floating particles from moving into the drainfield. Anaerobic bacteria works to break down both the **sludge** and **scum layers**. Gasses are generated in the decomposition process, which are vented back through the plumbing and out roof vents. Gravity carries the **effluent liquid** or wastewater from the outlet side of the septic tank into the drainfield. Ideally the **effluent** flowing into the drainfield should be nearly free of organic particles.

Single Compartment Septic Tank Cutaway (Side View)

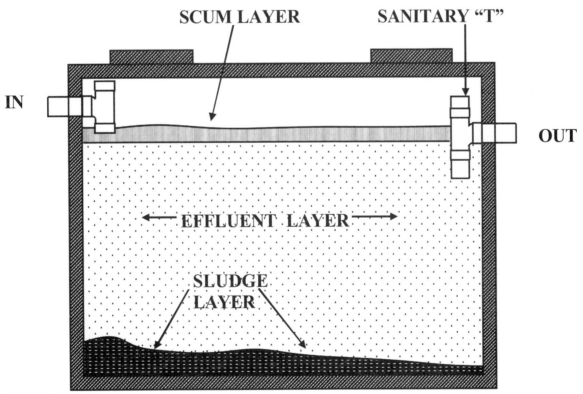

Fig. A-3

In most areas, newer septic tanks have two compartments (Fig. A-4), which are connected by a hole or short pipe, to allow effluent to flow through. The divider helps reduce the amount of organic material flowing into the drainfield.

Single Compartment Septic Tank Cutaway (Side View)

Fig. A-4

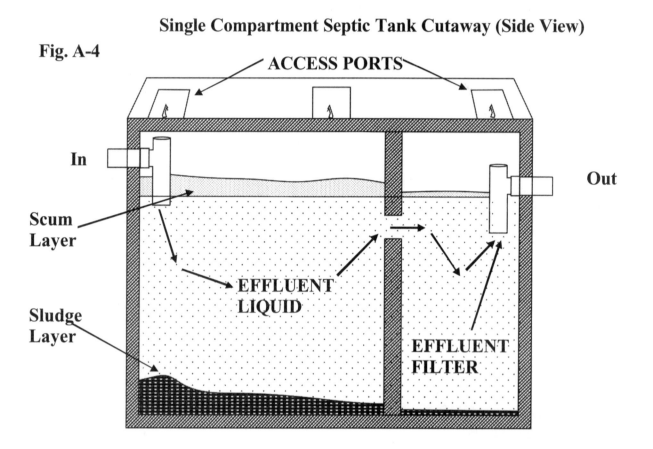

A second way to reduce the amount of organic material from flowing into drainfields is an effluent filter. The effluent filter is a plastic module which slides inside the sanitary "T". Effluent liquid flows up through the series of slotted baffles which removes much of the larger organic material. Fig. A-5 is a photo of a sanitary "T" and effluent filter.

Note: The filter is pulled up to illustrate baffles.

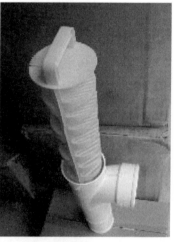

Fig. A-5

Drainfields

The drainfield, or leach field, **is an area where effluent liquid flows from the septic tank, until it can be absorbed into the soil.** There are several different types of drainfield systems installed today. Most older drainfield systems have a trench, about two feet wide and 3 feet deep, dug into the soil with a perforated pipe surrounded by aggregate (Fig. A-6). The aggregate allows liquid to flow freely from the perforated pipe over the entire bottom of the trench. Nearly all types of drainfield systems depend on the soil's ability to percolate or absorb the effluent liquid.

As liquid flows into the drainfield it carries bacteria and suspended organic particles into the pipes and trenches. As the effluent liquid seeps into the soil, much of the bacteria and suspended particles are filtered by the soil. **Over time the soil's filtering process builds up a layer of black jelly-like substance called a *biomat.*** The *biomat* layer breaks down slowly, due to the lack of oxygen and the relatively low level of aerobic bacteria. Some water seeps through the biomat layer, but the process is very slow. The biomat layer first forms

Fig. A-6   **Drainfield Cutaway View**

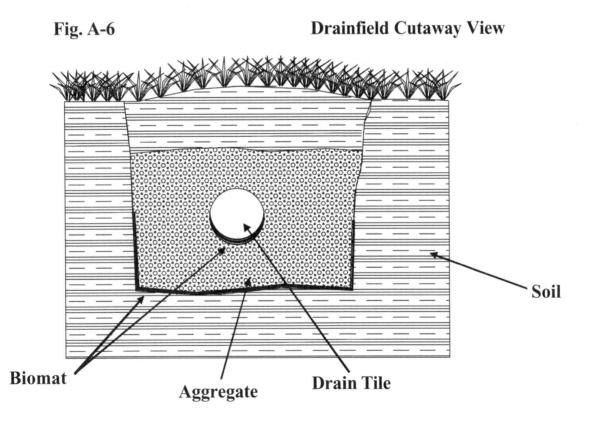

Biomat   Aggregate   Drain Tile   Soil

along the bottom of the drainfield trench, then up the sides and eventually reduces the amount of liquid percolation into the soil. **When the amount of effluent going into the drainfield exceeds the amount of liquid that can be absorbed by the surrounding soil, the result is drainfield failure. This failure mode is known as hydraulic failure.**

Septic System Problem Solving and Prevention

Drainfields usually fail at the worst possible time, like during Thanksgiving or Christmas holidays. This untimely failure is not because the holiday gods are angry with you for not getting into the holiday spirit back in July when you first saw Christmas decorations in department stores. This is the time of year when more cooking and dishwashing is done. There is less sunlight and heat to promote evaporation. Also, plants and trees have gone dormant and stopped removing water from the soil. All these factors contribute to adding more pressure on the drainfield and reducing the rate of absorption of liquid into the soil.

Although drainfields fail for reasons other than hydraulic overloading, it is the most common problem. It's important to have a basic understanding of the different failure modes and what symptoms to look for.

Drainfield failure will sometimes start out with sewage backing up and running out of toilets or showers in the lowest area of the house, or toilets may not flush properly. If the drain lines are not very deep, the failure mode may show up as a permanent wet spot in the drainfield area, which may be accompanied by a strong sewage odor. When effluent liquid flows to the surface, it is loaded with bacteria, nitrogen, and nitrates. There are many health concerns about bacteria and nitrates on the soil surface. These can come into contact with children and pets playing in the area, or may be washed into streams by rain as storm water runoff. The effluent liquid which rises to the surface will often form a layer of black sludge on top. **Failing drainfields play a significant role in the poor water quality of local lakes and streams.**

Septic System Recovery Mode

At the first signs of drainfield failure you should greatly reduce the amount of water flowing into the septic tank. If sewage is backing up in toilets, tubs or showers you should turn off the main water supply line into the house. A backed up toilet is a problem you cannot ignore, but you can assess the situation and evaluate your options.

Understanding your options when drainfield failures occur is your best defense against making quick decisions about expensive repairs. Start out by having the septic tank pumped by a qualified and reputable company. (Having a 2 page ad in the Yellow Pages does not necessarily make them qualified or reputable). Ask friends or neighbors about companies that have given them good service at a reasonable price. Usually if the person you talk to is more interested in solving your problem than cashing your check, they will do a good job. Septic tank service companies can usually make a fair assessment of the type of failure causing your problem. Some septic system service companies can run a high pressure hose into the drainfield, to check for blockage or tree roots in drainfield lines. The high pressure hose will clean the inside of the drain line, but does little to improve the quality of the soil surrounding it. If you have clay soil, more often than not, the final diagnosis is hydraulic failure of the drainfield. In some cases just shutting off the water supply and going on vacation for a couple of weeks will allow the drainfield to recover. Here you have to ask yourself; "Would I rather blow $6,000 on a new drainfield or a vacation to Australia?" Truth is, neither way offers many long-term guarantees.

Learn up-front the level of inspection and troubleshooting the septic system service company will perform while they are working on your system. The company should pump out the tank, then pressure wash the inside. They should remove inspection covers on both ends of the septic tank to allow inspection of the sanitary "T" or baffles and look for drainage into the tank when no water is being used in the home. If there is no water being used in the home, but fluid is entering the septic tank from the inlet side, more troubleshooting should be done to determine the cause. If effluent liquid flows back into the septic tank from the drainfield, it is usually due to hydraulic failure in the drainfield.

Unless you just happen to have a few extra thousand dollars Wall Street hasn't taken yet that you would like to donate to a company with a centerfold in the Yellow Pages, look at all the options you have. Some septic tank service companies will go straight for the jugular vein and tell you that your only option is a new drainfield. My advise is grab your checkbook and run. Follow the steps in the Appendix of this book to check for leaks in the water system which may have caused the failure to occur. Reduce the amount of water usage by taking laundry to a friend's house, take shorter showers and keep all other water usage to a bare minimum. Closely check the septic tank to insure that effluent is not backing up. After about two weeks of minimal water usage, try returning to normal usage and continue to keep a close watch on the septic tank. Often a vacation for your septic system will allow at least a partial recovery.

In most cases, drainfields don't completely fail to absorb effluent liquids, they just do not have ability to absorb the amount of liquids we pour down the drain. Adding even a basic graywater system can greatly reduce the amount of liquid flowing into a septic system, enough to allow the drainfield to recover. A graywater system can often be a very cost effective alternative to drainfield replacement.

Prevention of Septic System Failure

Septic systems often fail due to the lack of maintenance of the components that drain into it, or the lack of maintenance on the septic system itself. Here we will list a variety of things the average homeowner can do to prevent possible problems.

One of the more prominent reasons for premature drainfield failure is leaky toilets. Any constant leak into the septic tank will generate a constant supply of effluent liquid flowing into the drainfield. Drainfields need rest periods with nothing flowing in. Even short rest periods while you sleep or work are essential for a healthy septic system.

The average home loses about 14 gallons of water per day from leaking valves or toilets. Any evidence of leaks from faucets or toilets should be resolved immediately.

Here is a quick method to check for leaks in a water system.

- Shut off any items such as ice makers or humidifiers and any other device which may use water automatically.

- Gas water heaters should be set to pilot and electric water heaters should have power turned off. (Expansion of water being heated could give a false reading.)

- Connect a pressure gauge to a hose bib and open valve (Fig. A-7). Ensure there are no leaks around the valve or gauge.

- Shut off the main water supply valve for the system.

- After 1 hour check the pressure gauge. If the pressure has dropped significantly, further tests should be done to determine the cause or location of the leak. Don't be too alarmed at some drop in pressure. On average a 10 PSI drop in pressure will represent about 1 oz. of water. Also the cooling of your water heater may allow the pressure to drop a few PSI.

Fig. A-7

Note: The gauge shown in Fig. A-7 can be found in most home improvement stores. It is normally used to check water pressure before installing an irrigation system.

Tips On Toilets

As stated earlier, one of the more likely places for leaks to go unnoticed is the toilet. Unlike faucets where leaks are obvious, the toilet can have internal quiet leaks. Although some failure modes do make noise, they may go unnoticed for a long period of time. Checking for leaky toilets should be done several times each year. Here are some of the steps in troubleshooting potential problems.

Toilet Tank Cutaway (Front View)

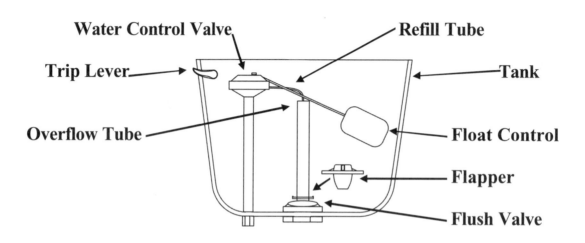

Fig. A-8

The most common type of toilet is referred to as a gravity-flow toilet (Fig. A-8). When the trip lever is depressed, approximately 1.6 gallons of water flows through the flush valve down into the bowl and on down the drain. A common problem with this type of toilet is a worn flapper or tank ball. This is the part at the bottom of the tank usually connected to the trip lever arm by a chain. With age (as little as one year) the rubber becomes brittle or develops a buildup of minerals from water. Either condition can cause water to leak around the flapper and flush valve, then flow into the toilet bowl. An easy way to check for this condition is to add food coloring to the tank then wait a few hours without flushing the toilet. After the time is up, check to insure there is still food coloring in the tank, but no sign of coloring in the bowl. If coloring is present in the bowl, the flapper should be replaced and the same food color test performed again to insure the problem is resolved.

Another common problem with a gravity-flow toilet is a defective water control valve. Often the water control valve will allow a small amount of water to continue to flow into the tank after the tank has reached the point where the water should be shut off. This condition is usually easy to recognize by water flowing over the top of the overflow tube and into the bowl. In some cases readjusting a screw on top of the valve will correct this problem, however this may prove to be only a temporary fix and should be monitored closely. The components to completely rebuild a gravity-flow toilet can be purchased for under $20.00. This job is not too complex for the average do-it-yourselfer. Excessive water pressure can sometimes cause these valves to fail. A failed pressure control regulator can allow water pressure to go up to a level that will cause water control valves to fail prematurely.

Pressure Assisted Toilet

Another type of toilet is the pressure assisted toilet. These are easy to recognize by removing the tank cover. The standard looking tank is just a cosmetic facade for the pressure mechanics inside. Pressure assisted toilets are a bit more difficult to repair, but determining if there is an internal leak is often quite simple. Shut off the water supply valve (usually located just underneath the tank). After an hour try flushing the toilet. If the flush performance is normal, there are probably no internal leaks. Open the water supply valve and the toilet should return to normal.

Drainfield failure can occur for reasons other than leaks within the system. Leaks are just an extra burden on a septic system that is already heavily loaded.

Here are some other steps which can extend the life of a drainfield:

- Septic tanks should be pumped and inspected every 3 to 5 years.
- Front loading clothes washers will reduce the amounts of both water and detergent flowing into the septic system, but not the amount of micro-

fibers flowing into the system. A top loading washing machine will use almost 50 gallons of water while a front loader uses just over half as much.

- Laundry should be spread out over several days of the week. Ideally you should only do 1 load of laundry per day.

- Newer septic systems with effluent filters should have the filter cleaned and inspected every year.

- Replace shower heads with a water-saving type to help your wallet, the environment, and your septic system.

- Garbage disposals should never be used with a septic system. They increase the amount of solids going into the septic system and quickly build up a thick layer of sludge in the bottom of the septic tank. If you do use a garbage disposal, the septic tank should be pumped at least once per year.

- Leaky faucets and toilet fixtures should be repaired immediately.

- Reduce the amount of cooking grease and oil going down the drain as much possible.

- Switch to liquid laundry detergent to reduce the amount of salt and fillers flowing into the septic system.

- Use only enough detergent to get clothes clean. Excess suds can indicate an excess of detergent is being used.

- Harsh cleaning materials or other chemicals should never be poured down the drain.

- Never allow automobiles or heavy machinery to drive over septic tank or drainfield lines.

Soil over drainfield lines should be slightly mounded. When the backfilled soil settles to become lower than the surrounding soil, rain water can pool until it saturates the soil directly over the drain lines adding more pressure to the surrounding soil. Fig A-9 is an illustration of a typical drainfield after the soil has settled. Some fresh water flowing through the system is helpful in bringing in bacteria and oxygen, but having a low area in the soil directly above drainfield lines will add additional loading to the system.

Fig. A-9

Drainfield Cutaway After Soil Has Settled

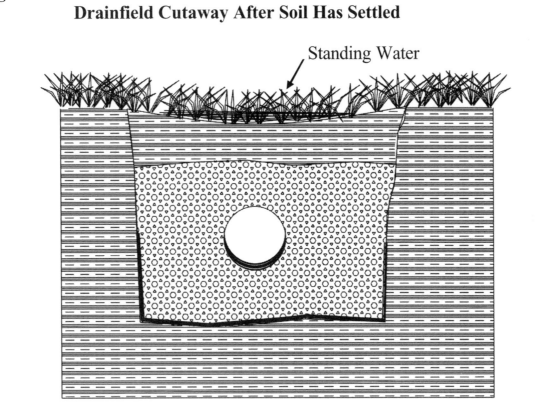

Standing Water

Roots from nearby trees can grow inside drain lines and eventually create a blockage that can prevent effluent from flowing through the drain lines. This condition can often be prevented by keeping trees from growing near drainfield lines. Some of the more likely trees to cause a problem are poplar and willow.

Note: Copper sulfate is a product sold to prevent roots from growing in drain lines. There are several problems associated this toxic product. Some areas prohibit its use without a license. Copper sulfate can leach into groundwater. If you do use this type of product, it should only be added to the drainfield lines or distribution tank between the septic tank and drainfield. Never pour it down drains or flush down toilets. Adding copper sulfate to the septic tank will temporarily kill all living bacteria in the tank. Although the septic tank will recover in about two weeks, this is a long time for a system to go with no bacterial action. Also very little of the copper sulfate will actually make its way through the septic tank and into the drainfield where it is needed.

Some companies sell septic tank conditioners or bacteria to flush down the toilet. There is little hard evidence that adding bacteria to a septic tank will actually do any good. In fact some studies indicate that adding certain types of bacteria may actually do a great deal of harm to septic systems and the environment. When in doubt about quick remedies for solving septic system problems, you can usually contact your local health department for information and suggestions.

Often drainfield problems can be eliminated by making a few changes in our daily lives. In many cases just understanding the problems that cause drainfields to fail will alert homeowners to make minor fixes before they need to spend thousands of dollars on drainfield repairs.

REFERENCES	
Wells and Septic Systems	by Max Alth, Charlotte Alth, S. Blackwell Duncan (Contributor)
Septic Systems Handbook 2nd Edition	by O. Benjamin Kaplan
The Grass Is Always Greener over the Septic Tank	by Erma Bombeck
Graywater Guide	California Department of Water Resources, P. O. Box 942836 Sacramento, CA 94236-0001
Home Energy Magazine Online July/August 1995	by Dick Bennett
Bromine	by Phyllis A. Lyday
Nursery & Landscape Production Management Basic Green March, 2000	Department of Horticulture & Crop Science Ohio State University Dr. Hannah Mathers
Using Graywater on Plants	NC State University A&T State University Cooperative Extension by David Goforth
Drought in Georgia Using Gray Water on the landscape	by Kim D. Coder
On-Site Sewage Management System	Gwinnett County 240 Oak St. Suite 101 Lawrenceville, GA 30045
On-Site Wastewater Management Systems	Dr. Larry T. West Dept. of Crop & Soil Science University Of Georgia, Athens
Greywater	by Carl Lindstrom

REFERENCES

SEPTIC SYSTEM OWNERS MANUAL	by Lloyd Kahn, Blair Allen and Julie Jones
PLUMBING	by Merle Henkenius
SOIL MICROBIOLOGY TERMS	by David Sylvia
Water Quality in Georgia Septic Tank Design and Construction	by Cecil Hammond and Tony Tyson
The Chemistry of Cleaning, Part 1	by Bruce Toback

GLOSSARY

acid soil– Soil with a pH value < 6.6

aerobic– Growing only in the presence of molecular oxygen as in aerobic organisms.

AKWADRAIN™- Prefabricated strip drain material used to collect or dissipate water into the surrounding soil. (American Wick & Drain Inc.)

alkaline soil– Soil having a pH > 7.3.

anaerobic– Growing in the absence of molecular oxygen as in anaerobic organisms.

bag filter- An open mesh bag which filters out strings, hair and larger particles which can flow down a drain but could cause problems for pumps or other components in a graywater system.

biomat- A layer of black jellylike sludge which builds up over time inside drainlines and soil as effluent liquid is absorbed into the soil.

black water– Water which contains sewage or other waste which may contain pathogens.

bromine- *a:* Chemical element: Br *b:*Used as sanitizer.

bromine canister- A container used to dispense bromine into water gradually.

clay– Soil particle < 0.002 mm in diameter.

surge/distribution tank- A tank which is usually placed underground, having one inlet and one or more outlets to temporarily store graywater until it can flow into a near surface drainfield.

drainfield- *a:* Leach field *b:* An area where drain pipe is buried for the purpose of dispensing liquid into the soil.

earth anchors- A device used to secure an object to the soil.

ecology– Science which studies the interrelations among organisms and between organisms and their environment.

effluent layer- A layer of mostly liquid which flows out from a septic tank as other liquid flows into the septic tank.

enzyme- Protein within or derived from a living organism that functions as a catalyst to specific reactions, like breaking down specific chemicals.

gravity sand filter– A process where sand is used to collect most particles while gravity pulls water through naturally.

graywater- *a:* Waste water which has not come into contact with sewage or food preparation. *b:* Water which has been used for laundry or bathing.

groundwater– Portion of water below the surface of the ground at a pressure equal to or greater than atmospheric.

hydraulic failure- A condition which exists when a septic system drainfield has more liquid flowing into it than the surrounding soil can absorb.

irrigation– Intentional watering of the soil.

loam soil– A mixture of different sizes of soil particles

micro-fibers- *a:* Lint *b:* Tiny particles which break or fall loose from fabrics.

near-surface drainfield- A drain field or leach field installed near the soil surface to take advantage of the soil's bacteria action and evaporation.

nitrates- *a:* An oxygenated form of nitrogen which can flow more easily through the soil than bacteria and other components of sewage and poorly treated waste materials *b:* The leading cause of ground water contamination from human and livestock waste.

"P" trap– A "U" shaped area of a drain line which holds water to create a liquid barrier to prevent sewer gas from flowing out of the drain.

pathogen– Organism able to inflict damage on a host it infects.

percolate- To pass through a permeable substance, such as soil.

pH– The degree of acidity or alkalinity of the soil.

phosphate- An organic compound found in some detergents as a cleaning agent, banned in some states due to its undesirable effects in promoting excessive growth of aquatic plants in lakes and streams.

poly tubing- A low cost pipe used in irrigation systems, unaffected by freezing.

sand– Soil particle with a diameter between 0.05 and 2.0 mm.

sand filter- A filter used to remove much of the organic material from graywater.

sanitary "T"- A fitting used on the outlet side of septic tanks to prevent floating debris from flowing into the drainfield.

sanitization– Elimination of pathogenic or deleterious organisms, insect larvae, intestinal parasites, and weed seeds.

scum layer- A layer of lighter particles which float to the top of a septic tank.

septic tank- A tank which is used in private waste treatment systems to allow sewage to remain stable for several days while the solids start to separate and break down by anaerobic bacteria.

silt– Soil particle with a diameter between 0.002 and 0.05 mm.

sludge layer- A layer of solids which settles to the bottom of a septic tank.

soil– Unconsolidated mineral or material on the immediate surface of the earth that serves as a natural medium for plant growth.

soil pore– *a*: That part of the bulk volume of soil not occupied by soil particles. *b*: Voids

Speed Leveler™- A device used to adjust the flow evenly from a distribution tank when there is more than one drain line attached.

storage tank- Large tank used to store treated graywater.

storm-water runoff- Water which rapidly flows over the ground surface during and after a storm, usually carrying contamination from human and animal waste into lakes and streams.

surfactants- Cleaning agents in detergents which keep soil and organic particles suspended in the wash water.

surge tank- A tank used to receive rapid surges of graywater until it can flow into a near surface drainfield or be pumped into a filter and storage tank.

tertiary treatment– A treatment process used to remove non biodegradable organic pollutants and mineral nutrients such as nitrogen and phosphorus salts from effluent liquid.

transfer pump- A pump used to move graywater from a surge tank into a sand filter and storage tank.

NOTES:

NOTES:

Mission Statement

The mission of Graywater Resource Inc. is to educate private citizens, business leaders and lawmakers on the value of using graywater whenever possible.

Graywater Resource Inc. will continue to research and develop more cost effective components and methods of installing graywater systems and improving storm water runoff.

WITHDRAWN